1940s

Library of Congress Cataloging-in-Publication Data

Hills, Ken.
  1940s / Ken Hills.
      p.   cm. — (Take ten years)
    Includes bibliographical references (p.   ) and index.
    Summary: Explores the decade of the 1940s worldwide, with an emphasis on the great war that dominated the news.
    ISBN 0-8114-3077-4
    1. World War, 1939-1945—Juvenile literature. 2. History, Modern—20th century—Juvenile literature. [1. World War, 1939-1945. 2. History, Modern—20th century.] I. Title. II. Series.
D743.7.H55   1992   91-43852
940.53—dc20   CIP
                                              AC

Typeset by Multifacit Graphics, Keyport, NJ
Printed in Spain by GRAFO, S.A., Bilbao
Bound in the United States by Lake Book, Melrose Park, IL
1 2 3 4 5 6 7 8 9 0 LB 97 96 95 94 93 92

Acknowledgments

Maps—Jillian Luff of Bitmap Graphics
Design—Neil Sayer
Editor—Caroline Sheldrick

For permission to reproduce copyright material the author and publishers gratefully acknowledge the following:

Cover photographs—Library of Congress; U.S. Army; National Baseball Library, Cooperstown, N.Y.; National Archives

page 4 — (from top) Popperfoto, The Hulton Picture Company, The Vintage Magazine Co, The Vintage Magazine Co; page 5 — (from top) The Vintage Magazine Co, Topham, Popperfoto, The Hulton Picture Company, Barnaby's Picture Library; page 9 — (top) The Hulton Picture Company, (bottom) Ronald Sheridan/Ancient Art & Architecture Collection; page 10 — Franklin D. Roosevelt Library; page 11 — (top) United Technologies Archive, (bottom) The Vintage Magazine Co.; page 12 — The Vintage Magazine Co; page 13 — (top) The Vintage Magazine Co, (bottom) Topham; page 14 — (top) The Hulton Picture Company, (bottom) Topham; page 15 — The Vintage Magazine Co; page 16 — Topham; page 17 — e.t. archive; page 18 — UPI/Bettmann; page 19 — (top) Topham; (bottom) The Hulton Picture Company; page 20 — (top) The Vintage Magazine Co, (bottom) Popperfoto; page 21 — (top) The Vintage Magazine Co, (bottom) Imperial War Museum, London/Bridgeman Art Library; page 22 — (left) Topham, (right) The Hulton Picture Company; page 23 — The Hulton Picture Company; page 24 — The Vintage Magazine Co; page 25 — (top) Topham, (bottom) The Bettmann Archive; page 26 — The Hulton Picture Company; page 27 — (top) The Vintage Magazine Co, (bottom) UPI/Bettmann; page 28 — Topham; page 29 — The Vintage Magazine Co; page 30 — (left) Barnaby's Picture Library, (right) Topham; page 31 — Barnaby's Picture Library; page 32 — Topham; page 33 — Topham; page 34 — (top) Topham, (bottom) The Hulton Picture Company; page 35 — Topham; page 36 — Topham; page 37 — UP/Bettmann; page 38 — UPI/Bettmann; page 39 — Topham; page 40 — Topham; page 41 — Topham; page 42 — Topham; page 43 — (top) The Hulton Picture Company, (middle) Topham, (bottom) The Hulton Picture Co; page 44 — Courtesy Harry S. Truman Library; page 45 — The Advertising Archives

The author and publishers would like to thank Trans World Airlines, Inc. for permission to reproduce the advertisement at the top of page 44.

TAKE TEN YEARS

1940s

KEN HILLS

RAINTREE
STECK-VAUGHN
L I B R A R Y

Austin, Texas

Contents

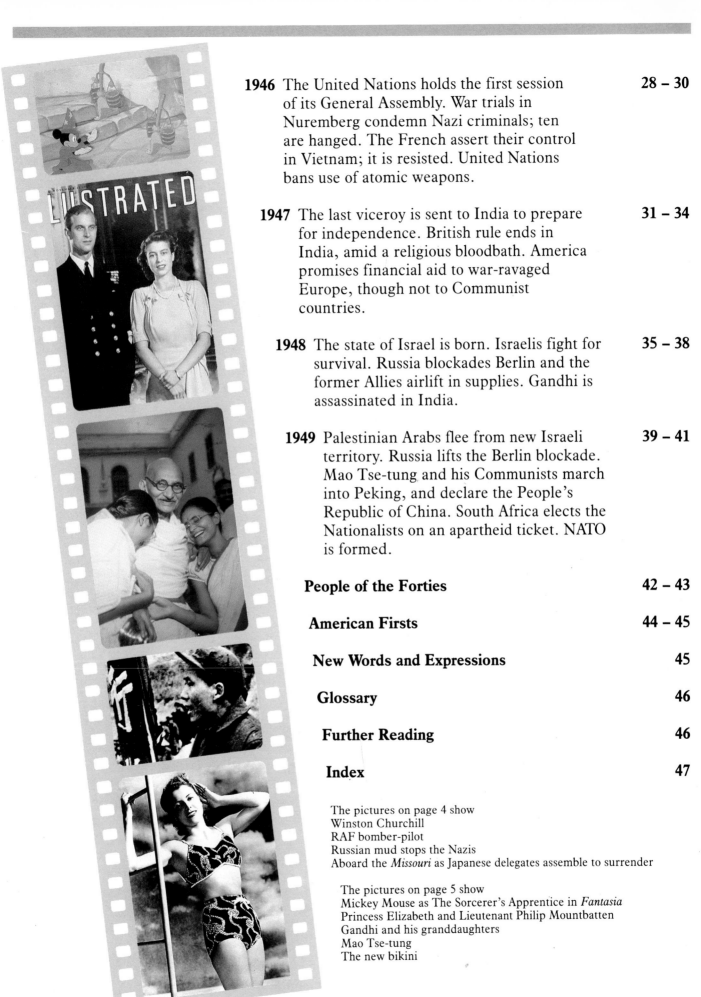

1946 The United Nations holds the first session of its General Assembly. War trials in Nuremberg condemn Nazi criminals; ten are hanged. The French assert their control in Vietnam; it is resisted. United Nations bans use of atomic weapons. — 28 – 30

1947 The last viceroy is sent to India to prepare for independence. British rule ends in India, amid a religious bloodbath. America promises financial aid to war-ravaged Europe, though not to Communist countries. — 31 – 34

1948 The state of Israel is born. Israelis fight for survival. Russia blockades Berlin and the former Allies airlift in supplies. Gandhi is assassinated in India. — 35 – 38

1949 Palestinian Arabs flee from new Israeli territory. Russia lifts the Berlin blockade. Mao Tse-tung and his Communists march into Peking, and declare the People's Republic of China. South Africa elects the Nationalists on an apartheid ticket. NATO is formed. — 39 – 41

People of the Forties — 42 – 43

American Firsts — 44 – 45

New Words and Expressions — 45

Glossary — 46

Further Reading — 46

Index — 47

The pictures on page 4 show
Winston Churchill
RAF bomber-pilot
Russian mud stops the Nazis
Aboard the *Missouri* as Japanese delegates assemble to surrender

The pictures on page 5 show
Mickey Mouse as The Sorcerer's Apprentice in *Fantasia*
Princess Elizabeth and Lieutenant Philip Mountbatten
Gandhi and his granddaughters
Mao Tse-tung
The new bikini

5

Introduction

The forties were dominated by World War II. It was the most costly and destructive war in history and its effects, for good and ill, were felt far beyond the battlefields. Over 55 million people died; about 15 million combatants, the rest civilians. Many of these died from bombing; more died in concentration camps, or from hunger and disease.

After the war was over, millions of people were left homeless. In western Germany alone, one in five of the population was a "displaced person." Some had fled from the east of Germany when the Russian army arrived; others were slave workers from countries Germany had conquered, brought to Germany to work. From all parts of Europe, Jews who had survived the holocaust flocked to Palestine in hopes of founding a Jewish state there.

The United States entered a period of great prosperity after the war. A soaring birthrate produced more consumers who fueled the economy. Huge clusters of homes were built in rings outside major cities. People flocked to these suburbs to find more open space, new homes, and often better schools. The move to the suburbs caused a jump in the ownership of cars, which were needed to get to jobs in the cities. This in turn prompted the construction of a nationwide network of superhighways. Along these highways were built motels, gas stations, and fast-food restaurants. Other industries that boomed after the war included electronics, plastics, frozen foods, and jet aircraft.

Throughout Europe, people's view of the world changed because of the war. The same was true in those African and Asian countries under the control of various European empires. In the first years of the war the colonial powers suffered crushing defeats. They were humiliated in the eyes of their colonial subjects. After the war, there was no going back. One after another, the colonies won their independence. The story of these new countries was beginning to unfold at the end of the decade. The European powers had lost their empires and owed vast sums of money to the United States, which emerged as the most powerful nation, along with the Soviet Union. The entire world seemed to line up on either side with one of these "superpowers," under the dread shadow of the atomic bomb.

YEARS	WORLD WAR II
1940	German blitzkrieg overwhelms Allies. Dunkirk miracle: British troops saved. U.S. military draft
1941	German army invades USSR. Winter halts German advance. Japanese attack Pearl Harbor.
1942	Battle of Stalingrad Japanese capture Singapore. Alamein: Britain's desert victory U.S. Marines fight for Quadalcanal.
1943	Kursk, the gigantic battle. Allies beat Axis in desert war. Hard fighting in Italy Japan: the ring begins to close.
1944	D-Day: the invasion of Europe Allies reach the Rhine. Japanese disasters in the Pacific
1945	Germany surrenders. Atom bomb destroys Hiroshima. Japan surrenders. End of the war.
YEARS	**WORLD AFFAIRS**
1946	First meeting of UN UN bans the atom bomb. An "iron curtain" divides Europe. War danger in Vietnam
1947	U.S. saves Europe with Marshall Plan. Thousands die as India becomes free. Truman pledges aid against Reds.
1948	East and West squabble over Germany. Russians blockade West Berlin. Allied airlift saves Berlin. Burma wins independence.
1949	Russians lift Berlin blockade. NATO alliance to protect the West. China proclaimed Communist republic by Mao Tse-tung. Apartheid established in South Africa.

OTHER NEWS	WARTIME ACTIONS	
Prehistoric pictures found in France. Stalin crushes all opposition. U.S. voters pick Roosevelt again.	**1939** **Sept. 1**	Germany invades Poland.
	Sept. 2	Britain and France issue an ultimatum to Germany threatening to declare war unless Germany withdraws. Germany does not reply. Within a week, the following countries declare war on Germany:

Roosevelt signs Lend-Lease Act. U.S. Wage and Price Agency created. Walt Disney's fantastic *Fantasia*		Britain and Britain's colonies
		   Australia
		   New Zealand
		   South Africa
		   Canada
		   France and all French colonies

French people suffer under German occupation. Fermi splits atom. Gas rationing in U.S.	**Sept. 17** **1940 April 9** **June 9** **May 10**	Russians invade Poland. Germany invades Denmark and Norway; by both have surrendered. Germany invades Belgium, the Netherlands, and Luxembourg. By the end of May all three sign a truce with Germany.
Slaughter in Warsaw's ghetto Allied leaders plan road to victory. Social security program in Mexico	**June 10** **June 22** **Sept. 27** **1941 June 22** **Dec. 7**	Italy declares war on Britain and France. France and Germany sign an armistice. Germany, Italy, and Japan sign pact. Germany invades Soviet Russia. Japan attacks Pearl Harbor.
Hitler survives bomb plot. United Nations planning meeting.	**Dec. 8** **Dec. 11** **1943 Sept. 3**	U.S.A., Britain, and Canada declare war on Japan. U.S.A. declares war on Italy and Germany. Italy surrenders to the Allies.
Roosevelt dies suddenly. Allies rule a divided Germany. China torn by civil war.	**1945 May 7** **May 8** **Aug. 8** **Aug. 15**	Germany surrenders to the U.S.A. and Britain. Germany surrenders to Russia. Russia declares war on Japan. Japan surrenders to the Allies.

WARS	PEOPLE	EVENTS
Palestine: British military headquarters in Jerusalem is blown up. Hindus and Moslems riot in India.	Nazi leaders executed. Goering escapes the gallows. Juan Peron elected in Argentina.	IBM creates electronic calculator. U.S. wage and price controls end. The "bikini" explodes in Paris.
British rule in Palestine to end. UN votes to divide Palestine.	Mountbatten: India's new viceroy London's royal wedding Car-maker Henry Ford dies. Heyerdahl's epic voyage	U.S. movie industry censored. "New look" in women's fashions Giant computer starts up. Spanish ask for monarch.
Last British troops leave Palestine. Jews declare state of Israel. War, as Arabs invade Israel.	Gandhi, India's peacemaker, killed. Truman elected President. John L. Lewis ends U.S. mine workers' strike.	Americans are big winners in London Olympics. Giant telescope dedicated in California.
Israel and Egypt sign treaty. China: Communists win civil war.	Mao Tse-tung, China's new master Orwell's nightmare novel *1984*	Gold Coast has new political party headed by Kwame Nkrumah, with independence as goal.

1940

THE WAR IN EUROPE

STALEMATE

March 3, London Britain and France declared war on Germany six months ago, when Germany invaded Poland. Their armies face each other ready for war, but so far there has been no fighting. In Britain they call it a Phoney War. The German name for it is "Sitzkrieg," the Sit-Down War.

WAR BUILDUP

May 10, Oslo, Norway German forces invaded Norway and Denmark in April. The Danes were taken completely by surprise and surrendered. There was fierce fighting around Oslo, the Norwegian capital. A Norwegian Nazi named Quisling announced that he now rules the country on behalf of the German invaders. Now, most of Norway is controlled by the Germans. British and French troops landed by the British Royal Navy have failed to drive them out. Both the Germans and the British have lost ships in battles at sea along the Norwegian coast.

CHURCHILL REPLACES CHAMBERLAIN

May 10, London Neville Chamberlain has been forced to resign as Prime Minister of Britain. He has been criticized for feeble leadership and blamed for Britain's failure to save Norway from the Germans. Winston Churchill replaces him.

GERMANS OVERWHELM ALLIED ARMIES

May 13, France Hundreds of German tanks are advancing into France. They have burst through the French defenses and are moving rapidly west and north. This advance follows three days after Germany's invasion of Holland, Luxembourg, and Belgium. The German airforce (the Luftwaffe) controls the skies over the battlefields. The French and British are making hurried plans to fight back.

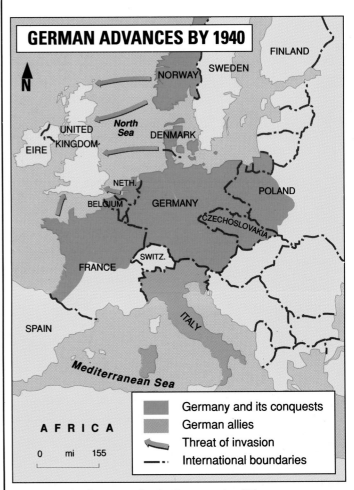

GERMAN ADVANCES BY 1940

Germany and its conquests
German allies
Threat of invasion
International boundaries

By 1940 the Germans had taken much of Europe.

ALLIED FORCES CUT IN TWO

May 29, France German tanks have reached the Channel coast and cut the Allied forces in two. The British army is trapped in the port of Dunkirk. The only way out is by sea. Hundreds of little ships are streaming across the Channel from Britain to rescue the troops lined up on the shore.

MAGIC DOWN A RABBIT HOLE

Nov. 1, Lascaux, France Some French boys out catching rabbits have stumbled across one of the most remarkable discoveries of our time. They came across a gap in some rocks, hidden by undergrowth. They climbed in and found themselves in a cave. The cave walls and ceiling were covered with brilliant pictures of prehistoric animals and their hunters. Experts say these remarkable pictures in southwestern France are about 15,000 years old.

A MIRACULOUS RESCUE

June 4, London The ships that went to Dunkirk have brought back to Britain over 300,000 men. Many of the troops have been saved but all their weapons and equipment have been lost. The British are without an army, but this successful evacuation is being called the Miracle of Dunkirk.

Allied soldiers line up to leave Dunkirk.

A bull and horses in Lascaux caves, France.

BRAVE DE GAULLE FIGHTS ON FOR FRANCE

June 19, London France has been crushed. Paris is in German hands and the French government has fled to Bordeaux. Further military resistance in France is pointless. But some of the French are determined to fight on from abroad. Their leader is a junior member of the French government, General Charles de Gaulle. The forty-nine-year-old de Gaulle flew to London yesterday. He was taken to see Prime Minister Churchill, and later made a broadcast appeal to the French people. "The flame of French resistance must not, and shall not die," he told them.

FIRST DRAFT NUMBER DRAWN

Oct. 29, Washington After a speech by President Roosevelt, Secretary of War Stimson drew the first number today in the military draft lottery. Government officials and members of Congress pulled other numbers at random. Men from each Selective Service area of the country whose numbers were pulled will serve a year in the army.

U.S. GIVES BRITAIN SHIPS

Sept. 3, Washington President Roosevelt told Congress today that he had made a deal with Britain to give them 51 U.S.-made destroyers. In return, Britain will give the U.S. 99-year leases for sea and air bases at eight strategic continental and island points in the Western Hemisphere.

NEWS IN BRIEF . . .

STALIN'S REVENGE

Aug. 21, Mexico Leon Trotsky, one of the revolutionaries who brought communism to Russia, is dead. Yesterday a young Spaniard plunged an ice-pick into his head.

Trotsky was expelled from Russia in 1927 for daring to oppose the Russian leader, Stalin. He finally settled in Mexico, but never ceased to criticize Stalin in his books and his speeches. Now Stalin has silenced him, for there is no doubt that the killer was acting on Stalin's orders.

MURROW REPORTS

Sept. 29, New York Americans have been riveted to their radios to hear firsthand reports about the Battle of Britain from C.B.S. reporter Edward R. Murrow. He has put himself in danger for these dramatic reports.

TRAGEDY IN THE ATLANTIC

Sept. 22, London The ship *City of Benares* was full of children. It was sailing to America to take them away from the dangers of war in Britain. Reports have now come in that a German submarine has sunk the *City of Benares*. Ships have picked up 46 children; 306 are believed to have been lost.

COMMERCIAL TV DELAYED

April 12, New York President Roosevelt announced today that the start of commercial television would be delayed while the Communications Commission develops rules to prevent any group from monopolizing the new medium. The rules should be finalized by the end of summer, and service could begin by September.

ROOSEVELT WINS AGAIN

Nov. 5, Washington American voters have chosen Franklin D. Roosevelt to be their President, for the third time. Roosevelt is the first American President to serve a third term in office.

STEINBECK WINS PULITZER PRIZE

May 6, New York John Steinbeck has won the Pulitzer Prize for his novel about the dust bowl, *The Grapes of Wrath*. A movie based on the book opened in January and received good reviews. It stars Henry Fonda and Jane Darwell and is directed by John Ford. Fonda gives a fiery performance as Tom Joad. The book's final chapter was omitted from the screenplay, but on the whole, the movie is a faithful retelling of the story of Okies migrating to California during the Great Depression in search of a better life.

Steinbeck expressed his liberal political views in this and other books, including *Tortilla Flat* (1935), about poor farmers and migrant workers; *Dubious Battle* (1936), about labor strikes; and *Of Mice and Men* (1937), which was dramatized the same year that it was published.

HELICOPTER TEST FLIGHT

Oct. 3, Stratford, Conn. Igor Sikorsky today gave Charles Lindbergh a flight on his VS-300, the first practical single-rotor helicopter. The military in the United States and Great Britain are interested in the helicopter's capabilities, because it can fly straight up or down, forward, backward, and sideways, and hover, or stay in one spot, in the air.

Sikorsky, a Russian engineer who moved to the United States in 1919, has been at work perfecting his helicopter since 1939. Others have designed helicopters, but officials in the U.S. Army Air Corps feel Sikorsky's model has the greatest chance of meeting government standards.

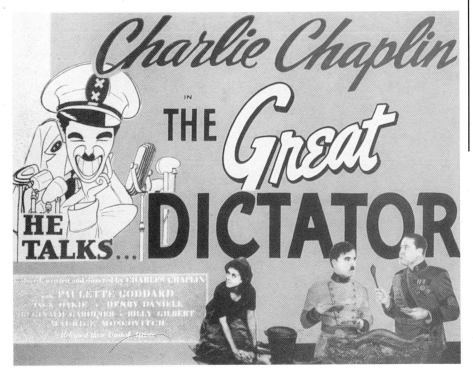

THE GREAT DICTATOR

Oct. 15, New York Charlie Chaplin's new film *The Great Dictator* is now showing. In the film, Chaplin pokes fun at Germany's dictator Adolf Hitler. He plays the part of a comic dictator, Adenoid Hynkel, dressed up in Nazi-style uniform, and made to look very like Hitler.

1941

RUSSIA INVADED

Oct. 26, Moscow In June, Hitler launched a gigantic attack on the Soviet Union. Three million men, with 7,000 guns and 3,000 tanks, poured into Russia on a front 1,240 miles (2,000 km) long. They soon overran the city of Minsk, 198 miles (320 km) inside Russia. Soviet commanders were bewildered by the speed of the German advance, and Stalin ordered that anything that might be useful to the enemy must be destroyed. Under this ''scorched earth'' policy, crops are burned, livestock killed, and all machinery destroyed. But the Germans heading for the Soviet capital, Moscow, are facing a new enemy—mud. Rain and heavy traffic have churned the dirt roads into knee-deep mire. Anything on wheels becomes bogged down. Worse is to come: the days are growing colder and the first snows are here.

INVADERS FREEZE IN RUSSIAN WINTER

Dec. 2, Moscow Thousands of German soldiers are frostbitten and their equipment is frozen solid. Hitler's armies are at a standstill. Fresh Soviet troops from Siberia, equipped to fight in cold weather, have joined in the battle for Moscow. They have begun a huge attack on a front 377 miles (960 km) long. The Germans are retreating.

THE WAR AT SEA

May 27, North Atlantic Battered by the guns of the British Navy, the *Bismarck* finally went down at 10:39 a.m. today. The huge German battleship threatened to create havoc among the convoys bringing essential supplies to wartime Britain. About 100 survivors have been picked up. At least 2,000 men have gone down with their ship.

The End of the Bismarck, by Charles E. Turner.

U.S. FLEET CRIPPLED

Dec. 7, Honolulu, Hawaii Japanese aircraft have bombed the U.S. fleet in a surprise attack on the naval base of Pearl Harbor. They have caused immense destruction and over 2,000 of our soldiers, sailors, and civilians have been killed. Eight battleships, three light cruisers, and three destroyers have been lost.

Japanese bombers create havoc at Pearl Harbor.

JAPAN'S BLITZKRIEG

Dec. 25, Hong Kong Japan has made spectacular progress since attacking Pearl Harbor. Japanese forces have landed in Thailand, Malaya, and the Philippines. They have seized the U.S. island of Guam and today, after a brave defense, Hong Kong has fallen to them.

WAR IN THE DESERT

April 11, Libya Earlier this year, British and Commonwealth forces advanced 500 miles (800 km) against the Italian army facing them in the North African desert. Germany's Afrika Corps has now replaced the Italians. Commanded by General Erwin Rommel, the Afrika Corps has launched a violent attack. Benghazi has fallen, and 20,000 Allied troops are cut off in Tobruk.

UNITED STATES ENTERS WAR

Dec. 11, Washington After Germany and Italy declared war on the United States today, Congress voted to declare war on Germany and Italy. Three days ago, on December 8, the President went before Congress asking for a declaration of war against Japan. He called December 7, the day the U.S. fleet was bombed at Pearl Harbor, "a day that will live in infamy." The only dissenting vote was that of Jeanette Rankin, Republican Congresswoman from Montana.

AFRIKA CORPS RETREATS

Dec. 10, Libya The Commonwealth 8th Army is advancing against the Afrika Corps. Tobruk has been freed and Rommel has been pushed back to where he started out last April.

WOMEN DRAFTED

Dec. 30, London An appeal for women war workers went out in Britain in March. Now, even more help is needed in factories and Britain has drafted all women aged 20 to 30. Some will join the services, others will do vital war work.

Women are replacing many male farm workers who have joined the armed forces.

NEWS IN BRIEF . . .

ROOSEVELT ANNOUNCES LEND-LEASE

March 11, Washington Roosevelt today signed the Lend-Lease Act, which enables him to transfer billions of dollars in weapons, food, or equipment to any of the Allies. The U.S. will be repaid in goods within a reasonable time after the war. Roosevelt has said that the deal is like a man whose house is on fire and whose neighbor lends him his garden hose.

WAGE AND PRICE AGENCY CREATED

April 11, Washington FDR has created the Office of Price Administration and Civilian Supply. The agency will keep prices from spiraling upward, discourage profiteering and consumer hoarding, and ensure equal distribution of products to civilians after military needs have been satisfied. The agency is necessary, President Roosevelt said, because the war is taxing the nation's economy.

DIMAGGIO SAFE AGAIN

July 16, New York Joe DiMaggio hit safely in his 56th game in a row today. This is the longest hitting streak in Major League baseball history. The streak began on May 15. DiMaggio is an outfielder for the New York Yankees. In 1939, he was named the American League's most valuable player.

AMERICA AND BRITAIN SIGN AN ATLANTIC CHARTER

Aug. 14, At a secret meeting at sea, President Roosevelt and Prime Minister Churchill have adopted a declaration of agreement on their aims in war and peace. The war will go on until their enemies have been defeated. Once peace comes, all people must be able to live free from fear and want under a government of their own choice.

The agreement to strive for a better future is to be called the Atlantic Charter.

Roosevelt and Churchill meet aboard HMS *Prince of Wales*.

THE BLITZ

May 31, London Nearly four million of the 13 million houses in British cities have been damaged by German bombing; 200,000 have been completely destroyed. Many thousands of people are homeless. They are living in any temporary shelter they can find.

FANTASTIC FANTASIA

Nov. 30, Hollywood, U.S.A. Walt Disney has made an entirely new kind of film. *Fantasia* is a concert of famous pieces of music, each one illustrated by a cartoon. In one, Mickey Mouse plays the Sorcerer's Apprentice.

1942

STALINGRAD THREATENED

Aug. 31, Stalingrad, USSR German tanks have entered the outskirts of Stalingrad. Most of the city is in ruins and 40,000 of its people have been killed in air attacks by the Luftwaffe. The German High Command is confident that Stalingrad will fall easily in a few days.

GERMANS TRAPPED

Nov. 23, Stalingrad After months of desperate street fighting, Stalingrad is unconquered. It is encircled by the Russian Red Army. The 250,000 German troops still fighting there are under constant attack and are dying of cold and hunger. They cannot hold out much longer.

Wrecked houses in Stalingrad lie under snow.

Ruins fill the heart of the city.

An abandoned gun awaits capture.

German troops advance through destroyed buildings.

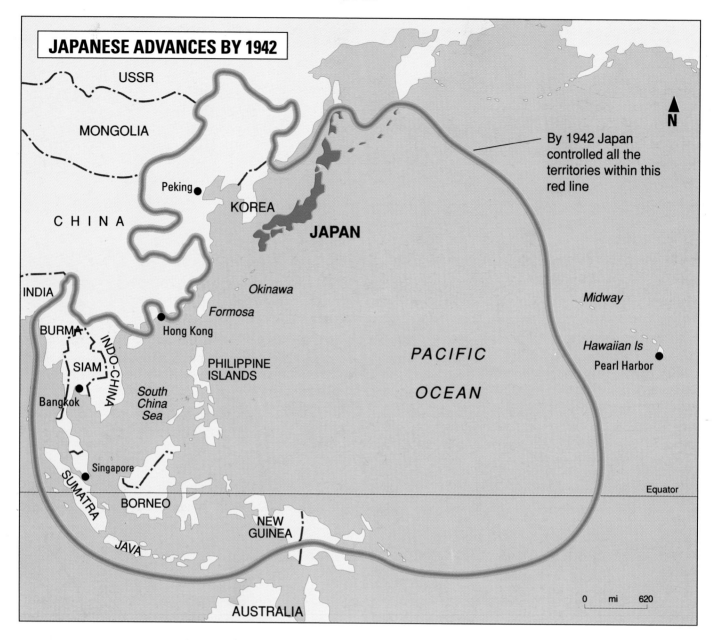

JAPANESE ADVANCES BY 1942

USSR

MONGOLIA

Peking

CHINA

KOREA

JAPAN

Okinawa

Formosa

INDIA

BURMA

Hong Kong

SIAM

INDO-CHINA

PHILIPPINE ISLANDS

Midway

Hawaiian Is
Pearl Harbor

PACIFIC

OCEAN

Bangkok

South China Sea

Singapore

SUMATRA

BORNEO

JAVA

NEW GUINEA

Equator

By 1942 Japan controlled all the territories within this red line

N

0   mi   620

AUSTRALIA

JAPAN MARCHES ON

May 10, Philippines Japanese armies have scored success after success in the Pacific and Southeast Asia. The Japanese force that landed in Malaya captured Singapore in February. The Japanese have also overrun the Dutch East Indies; they have occupied Burma and threaten India. Today the last U.S. troops have surrendered the Philippines.

BRITISH VICTORY AT EL ALAMEIN

Nov. 2, Cairo, Egypt After a 10-day battle the Afrika Corps under Rommel has abandoned El Alamein. This is where the Germans halted after a 137 mile (350 km) desert trek. The British 8th Army, under its new commander General Montgomery, is pursuing them westward.

General Montgomery confers with his colleagues.

A THOUSAND BOMBERS RAID

May 31, Cologne More than a thousand RAF bombers attacked the German city of Cologne last night. They caused widespread destruction. This is the first thousand-bomber raid of the war and easily surpasses in weight and ferocity anything the Germans threw against British cities last year. It is not likely to be the last.

THE LONG ROAD BACK

Dec. 31, Pacific Ocean Americans have begun the long slow task of driving the Japanese from the conquests that they have made since Pearl Harbor. In June, our ships and aircraft destroyed a Japanese fleet in a battle off Midway Island. Now, U.S. marines are fighting desperately to recapture Guadalcanal, one of the Solomon Islands.

NEWS IN BRIEF . . .

NUCLEAR CHAIN REACTION

Dec. 2, Chicago A group of physicists headed by Enrico Fermi has achieved the first controlled nuclear chain reaction. The scientists built a nuclear pile of uranium and graphite at the University of Chicago. The atomic pile is part of the Manhattan Project to build an atomic weapon.

GERMANS LOOT FRANCE

June 30, Paris The French people watch helplessly as the German conquerors continue to take everything they want from France. A black market flourishes but at prices only the well-off can afford. Food and clothing are strictly rationed. Disease among children is growing because of their poor diet. Few cars are running because gasoline is almost unobtainable by the native population. Coal and wood needed for heating are in very short supply and all but the rich dread the coming winter. The French are a beaten nation and they are not allowed to forget it. A strictly enforced curfew begins every evening at 8 p.m.

JAEGER

The best in Utility

DRESSING TO ORDER

June 30, London The war has hit the fashion industry. Trouser cuffs, pocket flaps, and fussy pleats will all disappear under the government's Utility plan. Any fashion details considered unnecessary will be done away with, especially if they use up too much cloth.

Some of the top names in the fashion business have been hired to design Utility garments. Hardy Amies, Hartnell, and Molyneux are among the famous designers who will dress the nation at reasonable prices. Britons may have to cut their clothes to suit the war effort, but they will still be stylish.

There are also plans to introduce Utility furniture.

JAPANESE-AMERICANS TO BE INTERNED

March 3, San Francisco An area including parts of Oregon, Washington, Arizona, and California has been declared a military zone. All people of Japanese descent, including American citizens, are to be evacuated from the area. The presidential order will affect an estimated 100,000 people.

Lt. General John L. DeWitt announced the creation of the military zone and said that those who are affected would gain "considerable advantage" by moving now, and "in all probability will not again be disturbed." The military said camps would be established to house the evacuees, but did not give the locality of the camps.

GAS IS RATIONED

Dec. 1, New York Gasoline rationing has gone into effect for the entire country. It will affect some 27 million car owners and five million buses and trucks. Car owners, with certain exceptions, can buy about four gallons of gas a week. It is hoped that the plan will conserve both gas and rubber tires. Thirteen states on the East Coast have rationed gas since last spring.

1943

THE TIDE TURNS

THE BATTLE OF KURSK

July 25, Russian Front The German invaders have suffered their greatest defeat in the Russian campaign. The German High Command planned to slice off a great bulge in the Soviet line at Kursk and trap everything inside it. A million German troops with tanks and aircraft were hurled into the battle but could not pierce vast Russian defenses. There was a triple ring of anti-tank positions, minefields, and fortifications around Kursk. For the first time in the war a Blitzkrieg-style attack has failed. It is a turning point in the war.

GERMAN ARMY IN RETREAT

Dec. 13, Russian Front Last month the Red Army retook Kiev, the ancient capital of the Ukraine. In the past year, the triumphant Russians have advanced more than 186 miles (300 km) and are halfway to driving the enemy out of their country. The Germans are in retreat.

INVASION OF ITALY

Sept. 10, Salerno The Allied landings in Italy are now complete. For the first time since Dunkirk, the Allies are fighting on the mainland of Europe. Italy surrendered on Sept. 8, but the Germans fight on. When General Clark's Fifth Army landed at Salerno yesterday, Germans met them with fierce resistance.

Amphibious "ducks" at Salerno, Italy, with supplies for the Allies.

VICTORY IN NORTH AFRICA

May 13, Tunisia The German forces in Africa have surrendered. General Arnim, who replaced Rommel in March, gave up the fight in north Africa today. Last month, leading troops of the two Allied armies linked up in Tunisia. The Afrika Corps was trapped between the Allies and the sea.

THE WAR AGAINST JAPAN

Dec. 29, Solomon Islands Japanese soldiers do not surrender; they fight until they are killed. One after another, the islands that ring Japan are falling to U.S. forces, but every foot of ground has to be fought for and American losses are very heavy.

GUSTAV LINE HALTS ALLIES

Dec. 31, central Italy The Americans and British have made slow progress up the Italian peninsula in the teeth of determined German resistance. They are now held up by the Gustav Line, a chain of German defenses across Italy.

BIG THREE IN PERSIA

Nov. 28, Tehran The three Allied leaders, Stalin of Russia, Churchill of Britain, and Roosevelt of the United States, are meeting in Tehran in Persia to plan the next moves in the war against Germany this spring.

Stalin, Roosevelt, and Churchill in Tehran.

NEWS IN BRIEF . . .

FINAL GHETTO ASSAULT

June 30, Warsaw, Poland On April 19, German troops entered that part of Warsaw called the ghetto, in which Jews have been imprisoned. The Jews, already wretched with hunger and illness, fought for a month until they were totally exhausted. Seven thousand Jews died in the fighting. The 56,000 who survived all this have been herded into new specially built concentration camps.

Polish Jews from the Warsaw ghetto are rounded up by German troops.

"ALL FOR ARMS AND ARMS FOR ALL."

THE THREE SALVAGEERS.

A poster showing salvage workers as the Three Musketeers.

A UNIQUE REGIMENT

June, London The 93rd Searchlight Regiment is staffed entirely by women. Their main job is to light up enemy aircraft so that British night fighter pilots can see them and shoot them down. Another task is to use their lights to show the way to badly damaged bombers returning from raids over Europe. One after another, the beams from the searchlight batteries beckon the crippled aircraft toward airfields where it is safe for them to land.

Women operating searchlights of the British Anti-Aircraft Command.

SAVE PAPER—SAVE CARGO SPACE

June 30, London No newspaper in Britain is to be more than four pages long. The government has issued this order to save paper.

MEXICANS RECEIVE STATE HELP

September, Mexico City Mexico is one of the poorest countries in the world, but it has just adopted a system of social security. If a Mexican earns wages regularly, he can use the system. There is free medical and surgical care, hospital treatment, old-age and death benefits, and free adult education. A poster in the new social security building advises: "Take care of yourself; Mexico needs you."

1944

INVASION OF EUROPE
EISENHOWER TO LEAD INVASION

Jan., Washington Last month President Roosevelt appointed General Dwight D. Eisenhower supreme commander of the Allied Expeditionary Force Europe. Eisenhower will head the huge Allied Force now assembling in Britain for the invasion of Europe.

THE GREAT ASSAULT

June 6, "D-Day," Normandy Early this morning, the first Allied troops waded ashore on the coast of France in the face of fierce German resistance. By this evening they had set up several secure bases along the shore. Allied ships and aircraft have been hammering the German troops and defenses.

GERMANS LOSE 60,000 MEN

Aug. 20, Falaise, France On August 2, American armored forces broke away from the Normandy beaches. They advanced rapidly and threatened to cut off the Germans still locked in battle with the British at Caen; 10,000 died in the battle and 50,000 are trapped around the town of Falaise.

The Landing in Normandy, Arromanches, D-Day Plus 20, June 26, 1944, by Barnett Freedman.

SOVIET ADVANCE NEARS WARSAW

July 31, near Warsaw, Poland The once-unbeatable German soldiers are in constant retreat. They were overwhelmed by the speed and power of the Russian assault when the Red Army began its summer offensive. The Germans have been driven from Russia and now hold a line along the Vistula River, close to Warsaw, the capital of Poland.

PARIS HAILS DE GAULLE

Aug. 26, Paris Paris is free. As was right and proper, Free French soldiers were the first Allied troops to enter the city. But today belongs to the man who has kept French resistance alive throughout the war, General Charles de Gaulle. Today, General de Gaulle led Free French and American troops on foot through 15 miles (24 km) of cheering crowds to the heart of Paris. He and his officers, together with a vast throng, then joined in a thanksgiving service in Notre Dame cathedral.

THE ITALIAN CAMPAIGN

Dec. 9, Rimini American and British forces have pushed back the Germans to a front winding across northern Italy and are now digging in for the winter. The war in Italy has become secondary. Allied forces here are being disbanded and many units are being transferred to the main battlefront on the borders of Germany.

SLAUGHTER IN WARSAW

Oct. 9, Warsaw It is believed that 200,000 Poles, most of them civilians, have been killed in Warsaw. When the Red Army reached the Vistula River, the Poles in Warsaw rose against the German garrison. They acted too soon. The Germans beat off Soviet attempts to break through to the city. In revenge, they massacred the Polish population and destroyed every building left standing in the city.

The ruins of Warsaw after the uprising.

SHOCK ATTACK STUNS ALLIES

Dec. 16, German border A massive German counterattack has rocked the Allied armies poised to cross the Rhine River. Early this morning, a huge artillery barrage descended on the American positions in the Ardennes forest. Tanks and infantry have overrun the dazed defenders.

GERMAN ADVANCE HALTED

Dec. 26, Bastogne, Belgium American paratroops have fought off every attempt by the German counterattack to seize this key town. The German advance is faltering as Allied forces prepare to recapture the ground they have lost.

THE GREATEST SEA BATTLE

Oct. 26, Leyte Gulf, Philippines In a battle lasting three days, the American Pacific Fleet has damaged the Japanese Navy so severely that it is unlikely to take a major part in the rest of the war. The Japanese losses are four carriers, three battleships, 19 smaller vessels, and 10,000 men.

Earlier this year, Avenger torpedo aircraft and the new Hellcat naval fighter won a great victory in the Philippine Sea. In a two-day battle, the Americans destroyed 600 Japanese aircraft and sank two aircraft carriers.

THE RED ARMY'S YEAR OF VICTORIES

Dec. 1, Belgrade, Yugoslavia As the Red Army advances, it is founding a new Soviet empire. As they drive the Germans out of the Balkans, the Russians are replacing governments friendly to Germany with puppet rulers controlled by the Soviet government in Moscow. Romania, Bulgaria, and Hungary have fallen under Soviet influence. A month ago, Soviet troops liberated Belgrade, the Yugoslav capital, where another pro-Russian government has been formed.

APPALLING COST OF PACIFIC WAR

Dec. 12, Philippines The U.S. Airforce is now able to bomb the Japanese mainland from bases in the Mariana Islands captured earlier this year. This success and others elsewhere in the Pacific have been won with great loss of life. The main strength of the Japanese Navy was used to crush the U.S. Navy at Leyte. The Japanese used "kamikaze," or suicide, tactics: pilots, dedicating their lives to the emperor, crashed their aircraft on U.S. warships.

Japanese kamikaze pilots; before their last flight.

NEWS IN BRIEF . . .

G.I. BILL OF RIGHTS SIGNED

June 22, Washington President Roosevelt today signed the G.I. Bill of Rights, which grants special benefits to veterans of the war. The benefits include $500 a year for up to four years for training and education along with $75-a-month payments for living expenses. Special interest rates for loans of up to $2,000 are provided for veterans who want to buy homes or establish their own businesses.

NEW PEACE-KEEPING BODY

Sept. 16, Quebec The Allies are planning for a better world when the war is over. President Roosevelt and Mr. Churchill have agreed to start work on an organization for keeping the world at peace. It will be called the United Nations.

HITLER ASSASSINATION FAILS

July 21, Berlin An attempt by a group of German officers to kill Hitler has failed. The bomb planted in his headquarters went off, but Hitler was saved by the thick wood of a table. Several of the plotters have been shot. Others are being held for trial.

BAND LEADER FEARED DEAD

Dec. 16, New York Glenn Miller, the famous band leader, is feared dead. His plane disappeared on a flight to France where he was due to appear. Glenn Miller and his orchestra have played in war zones in the Pacific, the UK, and Europe, cheering the troops with favorites like "In the Mood."

TEENS SWOON FOR SINATRA

Oct. 13, New York Thousands of squealing teens packed the Paramount Theater last night to hear Frank Sinatra, known as The King of Swoon or The Voice. Thousands more crowded the streets outside.

1945

WAR ENDS IN EUROPE

ALLIES ACROSS THE RHINE

March 31, Rhine River Both the Americans and the British and Canadians have made crossings of the Rhine. They are preparing for an attack on Germany which will link up with the Russians and end the war in Europe.

BATTLES RAGE IN BERLIN

April 24, Berlin The Red Army was the first of the Allies to reach the German capital, Berlin. The city is completely surrounded but the Red Army is being made to fight for the city street by street. Hitler and his closest followers are gathered in a vast underground shelter in the city. Hitler still believes that Germany can win the war, and gives orders to armies that no longer exist. He has about a million men to defend Berlin. Many are underage and half trained, some are old men, and all are short of ammunition. The Russians and their American and British allies have complete command of the war. The German airforce, so vital to the war, has ceased to exist.

TWO TYRANTS DIE

May 1, Berlin Hitler is dead. He committed suicide yesterday in his underground bunker in the heart of Berlin. Three days ago, his great ally Mussolini was captured and shot by Italian partisans.

A SUICIDAL DEFENSE

March 26, Iwo Jima This small rocky island, within easy flying distance of Japan, has finally fallen to American marines. Iwo Jima was defended by 22,000 Japanese soldiers. Of these, 216 survived to be taken prisoner. The rest died in the fighting.

Raising the Russian flag over the Reichstag, or government building, in Berlin.

GERMANY SURRENDERS

May 8, Rheims, France Yesterday, officers of the German High Command surrendered to the Allies at General Eisenhower's headquarters in Rheims. Today, they signed surrender terms with the Soviet Command at Karlshorst. The war in Europe is over. The war with Japan continues.

Allied soldiers liberating concentration camps were horrified by what they saw. This boy was at Belsen.

NEW YORK CELEBRATES VICTORY

May 8, New York The streets of Times Square, the financial district, and the garment district were filled with happy people from mid-morning on yesterday as news reached them of Germany's unconditional surrender. The crowd in Times Square was estimated at 500,000 at its peak between noon and 1 p.m. There were unplanned parades and singing. The first news of victory in Europe came at 9:35 when the Associated Press announced the surrender. The official proclamation from President Truman did not come until today so as to coordinate with announcements in London and Moscow. The celebration was mixed with concern for the war in the Pacific.

America goes wild on VE Day.

BELSEN CONCENTRATION CAMP LIBERATED

April 15, Belsen "Next day some men of the (Oxfordshire) Yeomanry arrived. The people crowded around them kissing their hands and feet—and dying from weakness. Corpses in every state of decay were lying around, piled up on top of each other in heaps. There were corpses in the compound in flocks. People were falling dead all around, people who were walking skeletons....

About 35,000 corpses were reckoned, more actually than the living. Of the living, there were about 30,000....

The camp was so full because people had been brought here from east and west. Some people were brought from Nordhausen, a five-day journey, without food. Many had marched for two or three days. There was no food at all in the camp, a few piles of roots (vegetables)—amidst the piles of dead bodies. Some of the dead bodies were of people so hungry that though the roots were guarded by SS-men they had tried to storm them and had been shot down. There was no water...

I went into the typhus ward, packed thick with people lying in dirty rags of blankets on the floor, groaning and moaning. By the door sat an English Tommy talking to the people and cheering them up. They couldn't understand what he said, and he was continually ladling milk out of a cauldron. I collected together some women who could speak English and German and began to make records. An amazing thing is the number who managed to keep themselves clean and neat. All of them said that in a day or two more, they would have gone under from hunger and weakness.

The next morning I left this hell-hole, this camp. As I left, I had myself deloused and my recording truck as well. To you at home, this is one camp. There are many more. This is what you are fighting. None of this is propaganda. This is the plain and simple truth."

(Derek Sington, political officer, reported by Patrick Gordon-Walker in *Book of Reportage*, Faber 1987)

DIFFICULTIES AT POTSDAM CONFERENCE

July 26, Potsdam The leaders of the United States, Britain, and Russia have been meeting to iron out how the new, smaller Germany will be governed. The leaders agreed to treat Germany as a whole in economic matters. They also agreed that Russia would receive a third of Germany's ships as payment for war damages. Difficulties arose over Stalin's rejection of calls for free elections in Rumania, Bulgaria, and Hungary.

SLAUGHTER AT OKINAWA

June 22, Okinawa Okinawa is the base that America needs for the invasion of Japan. It has taken three months of the bloodiest fighting to capture it. American commanders estimate that if the Japanese defend Japan as fiercely as they have fought for Okinawa, the final attack will cost a million American casualties.

HIROSHIMA DESTROYED

Aug. 7, Washington A new and most terrible kind of bomb has been dropped on the Japanese city of Hiroshima. It exploded into a gigantic, purple ball of fire. A huge, dark cloud shaped like a mushroom rose from it. The single atomic bomb was dropped by an American B29 Superfortress yesterday. Most of the city and thousands of its inhabitants have been wiped out by this new and devastating weapon. In a nationwide broadcast, President Truman spoke of the atomic bomb. He threatened the Japanese with "a rain of death" unless they agreed to surrender.

JAPAN SURRENDERS

Aug. 14, Tokyo On Aug. 9, a second nuclear bomb struck Japan. A large area of the target, the port of Nagasaki, was laid waste and thousands of citizens died amid the ruins. The emperor of Japan has told Japanese armed forces and people that Japan had no choice but to surrender to avoid complete destruction. World War II is finally over.

Where once the city stood, now Hiroshima is gone.

HIROSHIMA DESTRUCTION OBSERVED

Sept. 9, Hiroshima "Suddenly a glaring whitish pinkish light appeared in the sky accompanied by an unnatural tremor which was followed almost immediately by a wave of suffocating heat and a wind which swept away everything in its path.

Within a few seconds the thousands of people in the streets and the gardens in the center of the town were scorched by a wave of searing heat. Many were killed instantly, others lay writhing on the ground screaming in agony from the intolerable pain of their burns. Everything standing upright in the way of the blast, walls, houses, factories and other buildings, was annihilated and the debris spun round in a whirlwind and was carried up into the air. Trams were picked up and tossed aside as though they had neither weight nor solidity. Trains were flung off the rails as though they were toys. Horses, dogs and cattle suffered the same fate as human beings. Every living thing was petrified in an attitude of indescribable suffering. Even the vegetation did not escape. Trees went up in flames, the rice plants lost their greenness, the grass burned on the ground like dry straw."

(Marcel Junod, *Warrior without Weapons*, Cape 1951)

NEWS IN BRIEF . . .

SUDDEN DEATH OF PRESIDENT

April 12, Washington President Roosevelt died suddenly today. He was having his portrait painted when he complained of a blinding headache. Two hours later he was dead. Vice-President Harry S. Truman automatically takes Roosevelt's place. He has rarely been in the public eye, but those who work with him say that only Roosevelt knew more about the war than he does.

LIGHTING-UP TIME AGAIN

July 15, London The blackout in Britain is over. Streets, shops, and public buildings are lit up as they were before the war. Some children, who are seeing these bright lights for the first time, are said to be terrified by them.

HULL WINS PEACE PRIZE

Dec. 15, Washington Cordell Hull, the man Roosevelt called "the father of the United Nations," acknowledged receipt today of the Nobel Peace Prize. On a trip to Moscow in 1943, Hull got the United States, Britain, Russia, and China to agree to establish the organization.

CIVIL WAR IN CHINA

Oct. 11, China Talks between Mao Tse-tung and the Nationalist leader Chiang Kai-shek to unite China have collapsed and China is in the grip of civil war. It is ten years since Mao's Communist Red Army escaped from the Nationalists into northern China.

NATIONS UNITE FOR PEACE

Oct. 24, New York The United Nations has been formally established; 29 nations have signed the United Nations Charter. They hope to prevent war in the future.

DODGERS SIGN FIRST NEGRO

Oct. 23, New York Jackie Robinson is the first Negro to be signed by a Major League team, the Montreal affiliate of the Brooklyn Dodgers.

The logo of the new United Nations.

GERMANY AND BERLIN TO BE DIVIDED BETWEEN ALLIES

Aug. 2, Potsdam, Germany Germany is to be controlled by troops of the countries that won the war. A meeting at Potsdam to decide the areas to be occupied has just ended. Russia will take over the eastern half of Germany. The rest of the country will be run by the Americans, the British, and the French. The German capital, Berlin, lies in the Russian sector. It has been divided into four zones, each to be controlled by one of the powers.

1946

EAST-WEST TENSION GROWS

THE UNITED NATIONS

Jan. 10, London On this day 26 years ago, the League of Nations was founded. Today its successor, the United Nations Organization, is holding a meeting. Belgian Foreign Minister M. Paul Henri Spaak has been elected president of the General Assembly, but only by a single vote. He was supported by the United States and allies in the West. Soviet Russia and the Communist states of the East failed to get their candidates elected.

This difference of opinion is all part of the ill will and suspicion that has grown up between the wartime Allies.

BOMBING IN PALESTINE

July 22, Jerusalem Part of the King David Hotel, the British government and military headquarters in Palestine, has been blown up by a time bomb; 42 people are known to be dead.

The Jews want the British out of Palestine in order that they may set up an independent Jewish state. Some believe the attack to be the work of Jewish Zionist terrorists.

NAZI WAR CRIMINALS CONDEMNED

Sept. 30, Nuremberg,Germany The wartime allies set up a tribunal to try the Nazi leaders for war crimes. It has now announced its verdicts. Eleven war criminals, including Hermann Goering, have been sentenced to death; eight have received long prison sentences; two have been acquitted.

Prisoners await the verdict at Nuremberg.

WAR BREWING IN VIETNAM

Nov. 23, Vietnam French aircraft have bombed the port of Haiphong in the north of Vietnam, a former French colony. In March, France gave Vietnam its independence, but as part of the French union of nations. A resistance movement, the Viet Minh, has sworn to get rid of the French altogether. They are supported and armed by China. The Viet Minh controls large areas in the north of the country. The French attacked Haiphong to try to destroy the Viet Minh's main link with the outside world.

IRON CURTAIN FALLS

March 5, Fulton, Missouri "A shadow has fallen upon the scenes so lately lighted by the Allied victory ... From Stettin on the Baltic to Trieste on the Adriatic, an iron curtain has descended across Europe."

(Sir Winston Churchill)

EUROPE IN 1946:THE COMMUNIST BLOC

N

FINLAND
NORWAY SWEDEN
North Sea
DENMARK
USSR
EIRE
UNITED KINGDOM
NETH.
GERMANY POLAND
BELGIUM
CZECHOSLOVAKIA
FRANCE SWITZ. AUSTRIA
HUNGARY
ROMANIA
YUGOSLAVIA
ITALY ALBANIA
SPAIN BULGARIA
Mediterranean Sea

0   mi   150

— The 'Iron Curtain'
  Communist Bloc in 1946

GOERING ESCAPES THE GALLOWS

Oct. 16, Nuremberg Ten Nazi war criminals died on the gallows this morning. Missing was Martin Bormann, Hitler's deputy who disappeared in the last days of the war and has never been found. Hermann Goering also cheated the hangman. He committed suicide by biting a cyanide pill hours before his execution was due.

THE UN BANS THE BOMB

Dec. 14, New York All 51 members of the United Nations have voted to ban the use of the atomic bomb and other weapons of mass destruction. This decision expresses a great desire for peace.

The United Nations wants to prevent another destructive atomic explosion.

NEWS IN BRIEF . . .

THE "BIKINI" EXPLODES IN PARIS

September, Paris A bathing costume has caused a sensation at the autumn fashion shows this year in Paris. The outfit is very small indeed, and has been nicknamed a "bikini" after the island site of the atomic explosion test in the Pacific earlier this year. According to the designer, the bikini and the bomb have a similar explosive effect.

The new bikini has taken Paris by storm.

ELECTRONIC CALCULATOR USED

Feb. 14, Washington The United States War Department has announced today its use of an electronic calculator that is 1,000 times faster than any other calculator. IBM is the creator of the new device.

WAGE AND PRICE CONTROLS END

Nov. 9, Washington President Truman ended wage and price controls except for controls on rents, sugar, and rice. He said, "The law of supply and demand operating in the marketplace will, from now on, serve the people better than would continued regulation." Some prices may rise sharply, but Truman said buyer resistance will bring those prices in line.

ARGENTINA HAS NEW LEADER

Feb., Buenos Aires The rule of the army in Argentina is over. A free election here has made Juan Peron president. Peron has been a popular minister of labor in the military government.

Peron promises to give power back to the working people of Argentina. He will increase their wages, and nationalize banks and railways. He has also promised Argentinian women the vote.

HINDUS AND MOSLEMS RIOT IN INDIA OVER INDEPENDENCE PLANS

Aug. 19, Calcutta Thousands of Indians have been killed in days of fighting between Moslems and Hindus. The Hindus support the British plan for a new government of all India. The Moslems demand their own independent state.

The rioting was ended when British troops opened fire on the mobs. The situation is now said to be "under control."

Lord Wavell (left, pointing), viceroy of India, inspects riot damage in Calcutta.

1947

INDIA'S NEW VICEROY

Feb. 20, London Lord Louis Mountbatten is to be the new viceroy of India. He will also be the last, for the British government has made it clear that Lord Mountbatten's task is to steer India toward national independence. Power is to be handed over to the Indian people not later than June 1948. The country will remain a parliamentary democracy.

Lord Mountbatten was wartime commander of Allied forces in Southeast Asia, and is related to Britain's royal family.

MOVIE INDUSTRY INVESTIGATED

Nov. 25, New York Leaders of the movie industry announced today that they would bar from work ten professionals who have refused to testify before the House Un-American Activities Committee and are thus held in contempt by Congress. Their lawyer said, in part, that his clients felt that HUAC had no right to "invade the realm of ideas, whether manifested by speech, writing, or association." Last month, actor Ronald Reagan, president of the Screen Actors Guild, testifying before HUAC, said that the guild is not controlled by leftists.

IT'S A COLD WAR

April 17, New York Mr. Bernard Baruch, former adviser to President Roosevelt, has given us a useful phrase to describe the state of world politics today. In a speech yesterday in South Carolina, he said that relations between the Western powers and the Soviet bloc amounted to a "Cold War."

NEW LOOK IN WOMEN'S FASHIONS

Feb. 28, Paris Designer Christian Dior has caused a revolution in women's clothes with his spring collection. Women love his shapely dresses with long, graceful skirts that will soon replace the severe, square lines they have been wearing since the beginning of the war.

With good reason, Dior calls his collection the "New Look."

HINDUS AND MOSLEMS AT WAR

April 1, Delhi While the British ruled India, the rivalry between Indian Hindus and Moslems was kept in check. With independence approaching, the struggle for power between the two sides has led to violent clashes all over this vast country. The death toll is rising daily and the police and the army are unable to keep order.

THE MARSHALL PLAN

June 5, Cambridge, Mass. Speaking at Harvard University, Secretary of State George Marshall has outlined a plan to help Europe repair the damage of war. Billions of dollars will be made available to countries willing to cooperate with each other in order to bring about the economic recovery of Europe.

INDIANS AGREE TO BE DIVIDED

June 15, Delhi The leaders of the Hindu Congress party and of the Moslem League have agreed to the Mountbatten plan for the partition of India.

Lord Mountbatten proposes that the country should be divided into two states: a new state to be called Pakistan for the Moslems, and the rest of India for the Hindus and Sikhs. British officials are beginning the complicated task of working out the details of how India will be divided into two nations. They have very little time. Lord Mountbatten has decided to bring forward Independence Day to August 15.

JEWS DEMAND PART OF PALESTINE

July 18, Jerusalem The agitation for an independent Jewish state to be set up in Palestine is growing. The British ruling authorities are caught between the Jews on the one hand and Arabs on the other. Both the Jews and Arabs claim the right to live in Palestine. Jews worldwide were outraged when the British authorities turned away a ship crowded with 5,000 Jewish refugees from Europe, and refused to let them land.

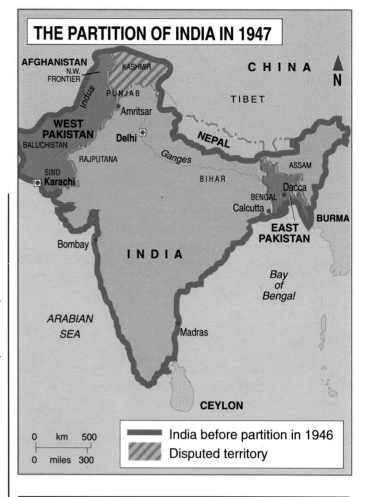

THE PARTITION OF INDIA IN 1947

- India before partition in 1946
- Disputed territory

NEW NATIONS BORN

Aug. 15, Delhi and Karachi At midnight last night, British rule in India ended after 89 years, and two independent states, India and Pakistan, were born. Pandit Nehru becomes the prime minister of India, whose population is largely Hindu. Moslem Pakistan is to be led by Liaquat Ali Khan.

Independence celebrations have been marred by clashes between Hindus and Moslems.

Pandit Nehru (left) and Mahatma Gandhi.

THE TRUMAN DOCTRINE IN ACTION

Aug. 31, Paris Sixteen European nations have met to prepare a response to the United States' offer of Marshall Aid to countries that are withstanding Communist sabotage and propaganda. They are asking for $28 billion over four years.

Neither Soviet Russia nor any of the Iron Curtain countries attended the meeting. They will not receive American aid. The U.S. does not intend to help the Soviets recover. The Marshall Plan is part of the Truman Doctrine. In March, President Harry S. Truman made a speech broadcast to the nation. In it, he challenged the power of the Communist countries. He undertook to support any nation against communism. This policy of international resistance makes plain the world is now divided into two hostile camps. The United States of America and its allies face the Communist countries led by Soviet Russia.

A German poster, which reads, ''An open road for The Marshall Plan,'' welcomes American financial help.

ROYAL WEDDING CHEERS GLOOMY LONDON

Nov. 20, London Princess Elizabeth, heir to the British throne, was married today to Lieutenant Philip Mountbatten. The wedding took place in Westminster Abbey. It was televised and broadcast to millions of people all over the world.

The bride and bridegroom are distant cousins. Both are descended from Queen Victoria. Lt. Mountbatten's uncle is Lord Louis Mountbatten, war hero, and now governor general of the new state of India.

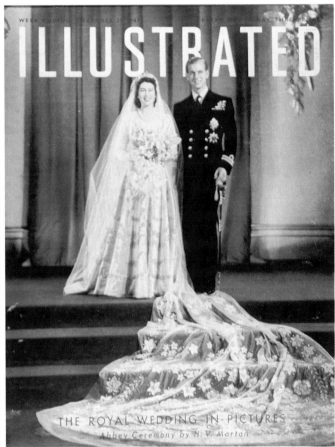

Cover story: the royal wedding

SEPARATE STATES IN PALESTINE

Nov., New York The United Nations General Assembly has approved a plan to create both an Arab and a Jewish state in Palestine. The Jews are in favor of the plan. The Arab states and the Arabs of Palestine oppose it.

The new states will come into being when the forces of the ruling British leave in May next year.

HUGE COMPUTER IN OPERATION

Dec. 30, Philadelphia The world's first all-electronic digital computer has been installed at the University of Pennsylvania. It has 18,000 valves, several miles of copper wire, fills a large room and weighs 30 tons. The computer performs complicated calculations at a dizzying speed. Already, however, work is going on to produce machines that are more compact.

INDEPENDENCE DEATH TOLL

Dec. 31, Indo-Pakistani border The final group of Moslem refugees from India has crossed into Pakistan. The division of India created over twelve million refugees, as Hindus living in Pakistan and Moslems trapped in India fled in terror to their new homelands. Over 400,000 people may have lost their lives and villages were destroyed in the turmoil that followed independence.

NEWS IN BRIEF . . .

HENRY FORD DIES

April 17, Detroit Henry Ford, pioneer of the motor car, the man who put America on wheels, has died aged 82. Henry Ford co-founded the Ford Motor Company in 1903, and by 1908 was mass-producing the famous Model T. His new assembly-line methods enabled the car to be sold at $500, making it within the reach of many ordinary American families.

Mr. Henry Ford beside his Model T.

THE KON TIKI ADVENTURE

Nov. 30, Tahiti, Pacific Norwegian scientist Thor Heyerdahl, with five companions, has recently landed on an island near here after drifting for 5,000 miles across the Pacific. The voyage began in Peru three and a half months ago and was made on the *Kon Tiki*, a raft built of balsawood logs. Heyerdahl claims that the journey supports his theory that the peoples of the Pacific came from South America, rather than from Asia as is generally supposed.

The *Kon Tiki* in the Pacific.

FRANCO'S PLANS FOR SPAIN

July, Madrid Since the civil war ended in 1939, General Franco has ruled Spain. But his brand of fascism is not popular. The United Nations has so far excluded Spain, so Franco is planning reforms. He issued a declaration of human rights in 1945 and this month asked all citizens whether they wanted a monarch on the throne. Most Spaniards said they did. Despite these moves away from fascism towards a freer regime, Spain will receive nothing from the United States under the Marshall Plan to repair war damage.

1948

EAST AND WEST AT ODDS OVER GERMANY

Jan. 18, Berlin The wartime Allies, the Americans, the British, and the French, have occupied the western part of Germany since the war ended. Now they have introduced a new currency in the parts of Germany they occupy.

The Russians have objected strongly. They claim that the Western powers are trying to make western Germany into a new state which will be on their side, and hostile to Soviet Russia.

PEACEMAKER ASSASSINATED

Jan. 30, New Delhi Mahatma Gandhi, the man who used peaceful means to make India free, is dead. He was shot today while on his way to pray for peace between Hindus and Moslems in India. His killer, a young Hindu, was arrested on the spot.

INDIA MOURNS GANDHI

Jan. 31, New Delhi According to Hindu custom, Mahatma Gandhi's body was cremated today. His funeral pyre was lit beside the waters of the sacred Jumna River. It was decked with thousands of beautiful flowers. Over a million mourners joined the five-mile-long funeral procession. The ashes were cast into the waters where the Jumna and Ganges rivers meet.

Police who have questioned Mr. Gandhi's killer say he belongs to a group of Hindus who violently oppose the Mahatma's message of peace and goodwill between Moslems and Hindus in India.

Trouble has broken out in a number of Indian cities following the Mahatma's death. Because of the violence, police were forced to open fire on rioters in parts of Bombay.

The ashes from Gandhi's funeral pyre were taken on a coach decorated like a temple. The urn went through a crowd of over a million mourners.

RUSSIANS CUT OFF WEST BERLIN

June 24, Berlin Berlin lies in the eastern half of Germany, which is controlled by the Russians. Today, the Russians have closed all the roads, railroads, and canals that link Berlin with the West. They hope that by cutting off supplies, they will force the Western powers to give up the parts of the city they occupy. If the Russians succeed in this endeavor, the whole of Berlin will be under Soviet control.

HUGE AIRLIFT TO BERLIN

June 30, Berlin The former Allies are running a huge airlift to bring essential supplies into Berlin. They want to prevent Berlin falling wholly into Russian hands. Cargo planes are landing at the rate of one every four minutes in the city, carrying food, fuel, and medical supplies.

The Western powers have no intention of giving up Berlin. "We are in Berlin to stay," says Secretary of State, George Marshall.

PALESTINE IN TURMOIL

May 15, Jerusalem Yesterday, at 4 p.m., eight hours before the last Briton was due to leave Palestine, the Jews announced that the new state of Israel had been born. Israel will have to fight for its life. Troops from five Arab nations, Egypt, Transjordan, Iraq, Syria, and Lebanon, are preparing to invade the new state. The United Nations is now responsible for keeping the peace in Palestine.

NO END TO THE WAR IN PALESTINE

Oct. 15, Jerusalem Fighting has been going on for most of the summer between Israelis and Arabs from surrounding countries. Twice the UN has arranged a ceasefire, and twice the two sides have used the truce as an opportunity to build up fresh stocks of weapons and ammunition. The conflict has begun again as Israeli troops attack Egyptian forces in the desert around the port of Gaza.

TRUMAN TRIUMPHS

Nov. 3, Washington Harry S. Truman has been elected President of the United States. Every opinion poll forecast a victory for his opponent, but Truman has proved them all wrong.

Mr. Truman is already the President. The office passed to him, as Vice-President, nearly four years ago. He moved to the White House as President when Franklin D. Roosevelt died in 1945.

BERLIN WILL NOT BE STARVED OUT

Dec. 31, Berlin The Soviet blockade of Berlin continues, and so does the Western airlift into the city. The quantity of supplies reaching Berlin is increasing as the airlift becomes more efficient, and as larger aircraft are used in the operation. Unless the Russians are prepared to risk war by shooting down the transport aircraft, the Western powers will remain in Berlin.

THE LONDON OLYMPICS

August 16, London After a gap of 12 years, caused by the war, the Olympic Games have returned. The 1948 games, held in London, have just ended.

The organizers were too short of money, and time, to build an Olympic village to house the athletes, or to construct new stadiums in which the events might take place. Americans dominated the field, capturing 38 gold medals. The United States won almost twice as many points as second-place Sweden and nearly three times as many as third-place France. A highlight was 17-year-old Robert Mathias of California who won the decathlon with almost as many points as he scored in tryouts, in spite of terrible track conditions.

FIGHTING AT GAZA

December 31, Jerusalem The Israelis are successfully defending their new land against the Arabs. They have almost cleared the north of the country of Arab troops and have knocked Lebanon, Syria, Iraq, and Transjordan out of the conflict. Fighting is now concentrated in the south of the country. The Israelis have entered Egyptian territory and have cut off an Egyptian army near Gaza. All attempts by the UN to persuade the two sides to call off the fighting have failed.

Americans sweep the women's springboard diving event at the 1948 Olympics. Vickie Draves (center) of Los Angeles is the gold medal winner.

NEWS IN BRIEF . . .

HUGE TELESCOPE DEDICATED

June 3, Los Angeles The Hale telescope, with a 200-inch reflecting mirror, the world's largest, was dedicated and used today at Mount Palomar. The telescope is named for George Ellery Hale, an astronomer who originated the project in 1927 when he realized that the growth of Los Angeles would interfere with observations made at Mount Wilson Observatory. The huge telescope is so well balanced that it can collect a million times more light than the human eye and will allow astronomers to study very distant stars. Work on the project continued in spite of Hale's death in 1938, although it was delayed somewhat by World War II. Mount Palomar is 5,660 feet above sea level, about 40 miles northeast of San Diego.

BURMA GAINS ITS INDEPENDENCE FROM BRITAIN

Jan. 4, Rangoon Today at exactly 4:20 a.m. local time, Burma became independent. Burmese astrologers chose the time and date in order to bring the new, fully independent country good luck. British control dating back to 1886 finally came to an end.

The Japanese occupied Burma in the recent war until British and Indian forces drove them out. The British returned but the Burmese were opposed to all foreign rule.

TRANSISTORS REPLACE VALVES

Sept., New York A revolution in electronics is about to begin and it is taking place in the United States. Our own Bell Telephone Laboratories has invented the "transistor." This tiny part will replace valves in radios. It is much smaller, can be reused, and does not overheat. In the future, radios may be produced that are small enough to carry around.

Researchers into the new science of computing also see the transistors as part of a major breakthrough in manufacturing computers that are smaller, more reliable, and economical.

COAL MINERS FINED

April 20, New York Although the nationwide coal mine strike ended last week, John L. Lewis has been fined $20,000 and the United Mine Workers union, $1.4 million. The strike was called off when union president Lewis won a major part of his pension demands for miners. However, the fines were levied on charges of contempt of court because of the failure of Lewis and the UMW to obey an earlier court order to return to the mines. Some of the workers still refuse to return to the mines in spite of fines and orders.

Striking coal miners in Pennsylvania wait for the order to go back to work.

1949

COMMUNISTS CAPTURE PEKING

Jan. 21, Peking China's long civil war seems almost over. The conflict between the Nationalists and Communists began more than 20 years ago. The Japanese invasion interrupted it, but since the Japanese left China after losing in World War II, the two sides have returned to the struggle.

Today, the Communist army led by Mao Tse-tung entered the capital, Peking. Chiang Kai-shek's Nationalists have been routed. General Chiang himself has retired, leaving the command of the Nationalist forces to younger men unknown to the outside world.

Mao's forces are now advancing to attack the last great Nationalist stronghold, the city of Shanghai.

ARMISTICE IN THE MIDDLE EAST

Feb. 24, Rhodes, Greece The Egyptians and Israelis have at last signed a peace treaty. The fighting in the Middle East is ended—for the time being.

The Israelis have won a great victory. Three-quarters of what used to be Palestine is now part of the state of Israel. Not enough remains to form a state for the Arabs who live there. Over 700,000 Arabs fled during the fighting. They live in harsh, poor conditions in the Arab countries around Israel's borders. About 160,000 stayed in their homes and are now under Israeli rule.

Conflict between Arabs and Jews is even greater than before the war. Peace in the Middle East seems as far off as ever.

Palestinian refugees leave their homes to seek temporary shelter.

A TREATY TO DEFEND WESTERN NATIONS

April 4, Washington Twelve countries from North America and Western Europe have signed a treaty to form a new peace alliance, known as the North Atlantic Treaty Organization, or NATO. If one country is attacked, the others will come to its aid. NATO includes the United States, Canada, Britain, France, Italy, Netherlands, Belgium, Iceland, Luxembourg, Norway, Portugal and Denmark.

The obvious purpose of the treaty is to make an attack by the Soviet Union or its allies less likely.

"WHITES FIRST" PARTY WINS IN SOUTH AFRICA

May 27, Pretoria The Nationalist party won yesterday's election on the slogan "Apartheid." It means "separation." South African laws already favor white people. Most non-whites do not have a vote, they may not travel freely nor live where they like. Under apartheid, they will become a separate race of second-class citizens. New laws promised by the Nationalists will make non-whites little more than slaves in their own country, one of the richest in the world.

MAO TSE-TUNG, MASTER OF CHINA

May 26, Shanghai Today, white victory flags are flying all over Shanghai as the Communists march in. The long battle for China is over.

Some cleaning up remains to be done, but there is no doubt now that Mao Tse-tung and the Communists are masters of China.

BERLIN BLOCKADE LIFTED

May 12, New York Russia has agreed to lift the Berlin blockade. A settlement was reached at the United Nations after lengthy talks between the USSR and the western former Allies.

This is a great victory for the West. Not only has the blockade been beaten, but the Soviet Union has agreed to the creation of West Germany as a separate state. It will be formed from the zones of Germany occupied by the Americans, the French, and the British.

There is delight and relief in Berlin at this news. Truckloads of food and other supplies are already on their way through Soviet-controlled territory.

NATIONALISTS FLEE MAINLAND CHINA

July 16, Formosa The last Nationalist forces have left China and have fled to Formosa, an island 60 miles off the Chinese coast. Here the Nationalist leader General Chiang Kai-shek is setting up a new independent republic. The General has given the island its ancient Chinese name, "Taiwan."

CHINA JOINS COMMUNIST CAMP

Oct. 1, Peking, China Soviet Russia has gained a mighty ally. Today, Mao Tse-tung has proclaimed China a Communist republic. He himself is to be head of the new state with the title of Chairman of the Peoples' Republic. His friend Chou En-lai is to be premier and foreign minister.

The United States supported the Nationalists in China's civil war. The Communist victory is therefore an American defeat. China's 540 million people are a huge addition to the strength of communism in Asia and throughout the world.

STEEP FALL IN VALUE OF STERLING

Sept. 18, London Yesterday a British pound would buy $4.03. Today, it is only worth $2.80. This announcement of a 30.5 percent drop in the value of the pound has shocked financial markets all over the world.

NEWS IN BRIEF . . .

BETTER SOUND – BUT AT A PRICE!

Jan. 15, New York Music lovers in the United States can now listen to their favorite works on new seven-inch "unbreakable" records. Unfortunately, there are two kinds of records, and they are made to revolve at different speeds. Our existing 12-inch records go around at a higher speed than either of them.

If people want to play the new records, which are said to produce much finer sound, they will have to buy expensive new equipment to play them on.

NON-STOP WORLD FLIGHT

March 2, Fort Worth, Texas The first non-stop around-the-world flight was completed today when an American B-50 bomber landed at Carswell Air Force Base near Fort Worth. The flight lasted 90 hours and one minute.

NKRUMAH HEADS NEW AFRICAN PARTY

Oct., Gold Coast A new political party has been launched in the Gold Coast, now a British colony. The Convention People's party, led by Kwame Nkrumah, aims to organize African people at village level. When they are politically ready, they will fight for independence from European colonials. They will use both strikes and boycotts–every means other than actual armed rebellion. After the liberation of his own country, Nkrumah, who studied in America, aims to bring all Africans into a peaceful union.

Race rioters and police in Durban, South Africa.

1984, A FRIGHTENING PROPHECY

June 10, London In his latest book, 1984, George Orwell makes nightmare predictions about the state of the world in the year of the book's title, 1984. There are three superstates in that world and they are endlessly at war with each other. There is no freedom. All activities are controlled; even thoughts are monitored, by the Thought Police. Those who displease the State are taken away to an unknown fate.

It seems Mr. Orwell had Stalin's Russia in mind when he wrote this grim portrayal.

SWEDISH NEUTRALITY SHUNNED

Nov. 10, Stockholm Sweden has recently proposed a defense pact with Norway and Denmark, the other Scandinavian countries. But the proposal has been rejected; Norway and Denmark are to join NATO. Sweden will remain neutral. At the end of the war, Sweden was a rich country; Norway and Denmark were both devastated.

RACE RIOTS IN DURBAN

Jan. 15, Durban, South Africa Over 200 troops and armed police are on guard in Durban. Riots started when it was claimed an Indian shopkeeper attacked a small black boy. Black Africans then took revenge on the Indian population, particularly the shopkeepers. Produce rotted in Durban market because Indian shopkeepers were too scared to go back to work. About 105 non-whites have died in the street fighting.

CANADA'S NEW PROVINCE

March 31, Montreal Canada has a new province. The former British colony Newfoundland has opted to join Canada, which is a thriving young country.

Although Canadians took an active part in the last war, their industry at home thrived. Canada supplied arms and food to the Allies. Steel and aluminum plants worked full tilt, and are still booming. Timber, fishing, and hydroelectric power are also very prosperous industries.

PEOPLE OF THE FORTIES

Dwight David Eisenhower 1890–1969

Eisenhower, or "Ike" as he became known, was a 1915 graduate of the U.S. Military Academy at West Point, and pursued a military career. He was appointed to lead the Allied invasion of North Africa in 1942. He was well liked by all ranks in the forces, and had a genius for making "difficult" people work well together. In 1944 Ike commanded the Allied forces that landed in Europe, and continued in command until the end of the war.

In 1952 and again in 1956, he was elected President. As President, he continued Truman's policy of resisting the spread of communism.

George Orwell, British author 1903–1950

George Orwell's real name was Eric Blair. He was born in India, went to school at Eton, and became a writer. None of his books gained him either fame or fortune until, in 1945, he published *Animal Farm*. All his life, Orwell attacked injustice and oppression, whether it came from wealth or politics. On the surface, *Animal Farm* is a simple tale about a farmyard. It is also a savage attack on the evils of extreme left-wing socialism. The novel *1984* followed. Its subject was the hideous conditions in a world run by oppressive tyrants.

Harry S. Truman 1884–1972

Harry S. Truman was a farmer's son from Missouri. He fought in World War I and later went into politics. In 1944 Franklin Delano Roosevelt chose him as Vice-President. A year later, Truman became President when Roosevelt died. President Truman faced huge and difficult decisions. He authorized the use of the atomic bomb to end the war against Japan. He led America to head the alliance of the powers against Soviet communism. In 1948, Truman was elected President for a second term. In America, the presidents who followed him frequently sought his advice.

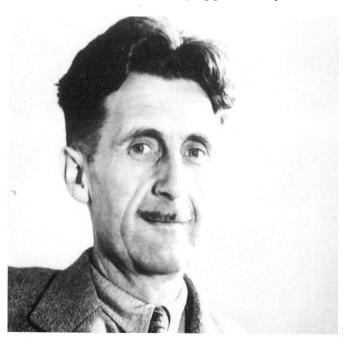

Winston Churchill 1874–1965

Winston Churchill was born to a British aristocratic family. His father was English, his mother was American. He became a soldier and fought in colonial wars in India and Africa. He went to the Boer War as a newspaper reporter. In 1900, he entered the British Parliament and was a member of the government during World War I. Churchill became unpopular after the war. Many thought him a dangerous warmonger because of his constant warnings of the threat posed by Soviet communism and, later, by Nazi Germany. In 1940, aged 66, Churchill became Prime Minister and led the British to victory in World War II. He was voted out of power in 1945 and turned to writing. He won the Nobel Prize for Literature in 1953. He became Prime Minister again in 1951, but resigned because of ill health in 1955.

Charles de Gaulle 1890–1970

A hero of World War I, de Gaulle fled to England when the Germans conquered France in 1940. From London he organized the Free French in resistance to the Germans. In 1944 he led French forces in triumph through the streets of Paris when the Allies liberated the city. He held France together in the troubled times after the war and later became president of his country.

Douglas MacArthur, soldier 1880–1964

MacArthur was commander of the Allied forces in the Southwest Pacific during World War II. He graduated from West Point in 1917 with one of the highest academic records in the school's history. He fought in World War I and received many decorations. In World War II when the Japanese forced MacArthur out of the Philippines in March 1942, he made a now famous pledge: "I shall return." He carried out his pledge in October 1944, when he and his forces landed on the Philippine island of Leyte. From 1945 to 1951, MacArthur directed the Allied occupation of Japan. MacArthur headed the UN command to defend South Korea until he was recalled by Truman.

American Firsts

1940 Congress passed Selective Service Act.
First black army officer appointed.
American illiteracy reached low of 4 percent.
First air raid shelter built, Fleetwood, Pa.
Writer John Steinbeck won Pulitzer Prize
  for fiction.

1941 Grand Coulee Dam, Washington State, began to
  function.
Ford Motor Co. signed a labor union contract.
Purple Heart medal awarded to a nurse.

1942 First jet plane tested.
Gas rationed nationwide.

1943 First Chinese became American citizen.
Pentagon completed.
Chicago's first subway opened.
Shoe rationing began.
First all-woman fire department begun,
  Ashville, N.Y.

1944 Paperback books published.
First jet fighter plane flown.
Ralph Bunche was first black State
  Department official.

1945 First atomic bomb tested, Alamogordo Air
  Base, N.M.
First Commission Against Discrimination
  established, New York State.
Nationwide dimout ordered to save fuel.
First railroad car with observation dome in use.
First municipal water supply fluoridated, Grand
  Rapids, Mich.

1946 President Truman announces Philippine
  independence.
First electric blanket made, Petersburg, Va.
First electronic computer completed,
  Philadelphia, Pa.
First artificial snow produced, Mount
  Greylock, Mass.
Buckminster Fuller designed house for
  mass-production.

1947	First World Series baseball game televised.
	First ballistic missile rocket fired.
	First aircraft flown faster than speed of sound.

1948	Polaroid Land Camera, first to make instant prints, went on sale.
	People lived in completely solar-heated house, Dover, Mass.
	Supreme Court declared religious education in public schools a violation of First Amendment.

1949	Frank Lloyd Wright wins architecture prize.
	Congress names June 14 "Flag Day."
	Discovery of cortisone arthritis treatment announced.
	First rocket to reach outer space fired, N.M.

New words and expressions

The English language is always changing. New words are added to it, and old words are used in new ways. Wartime activities introduced many words during World War II. Some of them are included in this list of words and expressions that first appeared or first came into popular use in the 1940s.

airstrip	ID card
bebop	jeep
blitz	keypunch
bug	like gangbusters
car pool	litterbug
crash land	microfiche
cannibalize	napalm
D-Day	on-the-job training
dirty pool	pinup girl
fifth column	point of no return
flak	portal-to-portal
fringe benefit	quiz show
flip side	radar
flying saucer	road block
freebie	rumpus room
gobbledygook	shoot-out
green thumb	walkie-talkie
gremlin	wolf-whistle

How many of these words and expressions do we still use today? Do you know what they all mean?

Glossary

armistice: an agreement between opposing sides to stop fighting.

armor: toughening to the sides of tanks, ships, and aircraft to protect them.

Axis: the Axis powers in World War II were Germany and its allies.

Balkans: a group of countries in southeastern Europe: Bulgaria, Hungary, Greece, Romania, Albania, and Yugoslavia.

barrage: a large number of guns shelling the same target together.

battleship: a large warship, usually over 30,000 tons, protected by thick armor and armed with a number of heavy guns.

blitzkrieg: a violent attack by land and air forces intended to win a quick victory. A German word meaning "lightning war." The shortened form "blitz" means the night attacks on British cities by the German airforce.

carrier: short for aircraft carrier.

convoy: a number of merchant ships traveling together, under the protection of warships.

curfew: a regulation requiring people to stay indoors at particular times, usually at night.

duration: short for "duration of the war," which means "as long as the war lasts."

Indochina: an area in Southeast Asia consisting of the states of Vietnam, Laos, and Cambodia.

Luftwaffe: the German airforce; in German *Luftwaffe* means "air weapon."

marines: troops trained to fight on land or sea.

partition: to partition a country is to divide it into parts, with separate governments.

"Red": another word for "Communist." Russia was for many years a Communist country and its army was often called the "Red Army."

Russian Revolution: the revolution of 1917 which made the Communists the rulers of Russia.

Singapore: a large port on an island at the southern tip of the Malay peninsula. In the forties, Singapore was part of the British Commonwealth. It was a huge naval base which was vital to the defense of British territory and trade in Southeast Asia.

Tobruk: a port in Libya on the Mediterranean. Tobruk changed hands four times during World War II in North Africa. Both the Axis and the Allied armies used it as a supply base.

Ukraine: once a large region of the Soviet Union north of the Black Sea, it recently declared its independence. It is rich in coal and minerals, and is the largest wheat-growing area in Europe. Hitler invaded the Soviet Union largely to gain control of the wealth of the Ukraine.

United Nations: an international organization set up during the war by the Allies to keep peace in the world once the war was over.

White House: the official residence, in Washington, of the President of the United States.

Zionist: in the forties, a Zionist was a Jew who supported the setting up of an independent state for Jews in Palestine.

Further Reading

Allen, Eleanor, *Wartime Children, Nineteen Thirty-Nine to Nineteen Forty-Five*. Dufour Editions, 1978

Bradley, Catherine. *Hitler and the Third Reich*. Watts, 1990

Cairns, Trevor. *Twentieth Century*. Lerner, 1984

Carey, Helen and Greenberg, Judith. *How to Read a Newspaper*. Watts, 1983

——*How to Use Primary Sources*. Watts, 1983

Davis, Daniel S. *Behind Barbed Wire: The Imprisonment of Japanese Americans During World War II*. Dutton, 1982

Leavell, Perry. *Harry Truman*. Chelsea House, 1988

Sandberg, Peter S. *Dwight D. Eisenhower*. Chelsea House, 1986

Shapiro, William E. *Pearl Harbor*. Watts, 1984

Index